Guide to Social Media Marketing 2024

Strategies and Tools for Growing Your Online Presence

Mark S. Brock

All rights reserved. No part of this publication may be reproduced, distributed, or transmitted in any form or by any means, including photocopying, recording, or other electronic or mechanical methods, without the prior written permission of the publisher, except in the case of brief quotations embodied in critical reviews and certain other noncommercial uses permitted by copyright law.

TABLE OF CONTENT

Introduction...3
Chapter 1..11
   Introduction to Social Media Marketing in 2024
Chapter 2... 25
   Setting Goals and Objectives
Chapter 3... 38
   Target Audience Identification
Chapter 4... 52
   Platform Selection and Optimization
Chapter 5... 68
   Content Strategy and Creation
Chapter 6... 82
   Community Engagement and Management
Chapter 7... 96
   Paid Advertising and Promotion
Chapter 8:..111
   Analytics and Measurement
Chapter 9... 126
   Adaptation and Innovation
Chapter 10... 138
   Case Studies and Success Stories
Conclusion.. 152
   Navigating the Future of Social Media Marketing

Introduction

In a world where digital connectivity reigns supreme, social media has become the cornerstone of modern marketing strategies. For entrepreneurs and businesses alike, mastering the art of social media marketing is no longer just an option—it's a necessity. But with algorithms constantly changing and platforms evolving at lightning speed, staying ahead of the curve can feel like an uphill battle.

Jake, a budding entrepreneur, was struggling to make his mark in the competitive world of online business. His social media presence was lackluster, and he couldn't seem to attract the attention of his target audience. Frustrated and feeling defeated, Jake stumbled upon a book titled "Guide to Social Media Marketing 2024." Intrigued, he decided to give it a read.

As Jake delved into the book, he discovered a treasure trove of valuable insights and practical strategies. From setting clear objectives to identifying his ideal audience, the book provided him with a roadmap for success. With each chapter, Jake gained a deeper understanding of how to leverage social media to grow his business.

Armed with newfound knowledge, Jake began implementing the book's recommendations. He revamped his social media profiles, crafted engaging content, and started actively engaging with his audience. The results were immediate and astounding. His follower count began to soar, and he noticed a significant increase in engagement and interaction on his posts.

But the real game-changer came when Jake delved into the chapter on paid advertising and promotion. With careful planning and strategic execution, he launched targeted ad campaigns that yielded impressive returns on investment. Suddenly, Jake's business was gaining traction like never before.

As word of Jake's success spread, his friends and colleagues took notice. They were amazed by the transformation in his social media presence and wanted to know his secret. Jake didn't hesitate to recommend the book that had been instrumental in his success. Soon, he found himself sharing tips and strategies from the book with millions of people around him.

Months passed, and Jake's business continued to thrive. Thanks to the strategies outlined in the book, he was able to navigate the ever-changing landscape of social media with ease.

What had once seemed like an insurmountable challenge had become second nature to him.

Reflecting on his journey, Jake realized just how far he had come. From a struggling entrepreneur to a social media maven, he owed it all to the invaluable guidance of "Guide to Social Media Marketing 2024." And as he looked towards the future, Jake knew that the lessons he had learned from the book would continue to shape his success for years to come.

Enter "Guide to Social Media Marketing 2024." This book is more than just a manual—it's a roadmap to success in the ever-changing landscape of online marketing. Drawing on the latest trends and insights, this comprehensive guide provides readers with the tools and strategies they need to thrive in the digital age.

At the heart of this book is a simple yet powerful premise: that with the right approach, anyone can harness the power of social media to grow their business and connect with their audience in meaningful ways. But don't just take our word for it—let the success story of Jake, a fictional entrepreneur, serve as inspiration.

Like many aspiring business owners, Jake found himself struggling to make an impact in the crowded online marketplace. Despite his best efforts, his social media presence was lackluster, and he couldn't seem to attract the attention of his target audience. But all of that changed when he discovered "Guide to Social Media Marketing 2024."

As Jake delved into the pages of the book, he was introduced to a wealth of actionable insights and proven strategies. From setting clear objectives to crafting compelling content, each chapter provided him with the tools he needed to transform his social media presence from mediocre to magnificent.

Armed with newfound knowledge, Jake began implementing the book's recommendations with remarkable results. His follower count skyrocketed, engagement on his posts soared, and his business began to thrive in ways he had never imagined. And as word of his success spread, Jake became a beacon of inspiration for millions of others struggling to navigate the complexities of social media marketing.

But Jake's journey is just one example of the transformative power of this book. Whether you're a seasoned marketer looking to stay ahead of the curve or a newcomer seeking guidance in the world of social media, "Guide to

Social Media Marketing 2024" has something to offer everyone.

So, if you're ready to unlock the full potential of social media and take your business to new heights, dive into the pages of this book and prepare to embark on an exhilarating journey of growth and success. The world of social media marketing is waiting—are you ready to seize it?

Chapter 1

Introduction to Social Media Marketing in 2024

- **Understanding the Current Landscape**

In the vibrant and dynamic world of digital marketing, social media stands as a powerful pillar, continuously evolving and reshaping how businesses interact with consumers. As we step into 2024, the landscape of social media marketing has grown more complex and, simultaneously, more essential for business success. Understanding this current landscape is crucial for anyone aiming to leverage these platforms effectively.

- **The Evolution of Social Media Platforms**

The social media platforms we rely on today have undergone significant transformations over the past few years. Facebook, Instagram, Twitter, LinkedIn, and emerging platforms like TikTok and Clubhouse have continually adapted to the changing needs of their users and advancements in technology. These changes have led to more sophisticated algorithms, a higher emphasis on video content, and the integration of e-commerce features directly within the platforms.

For instance, Instagram's algorithm now prioritizes Reels, their short-form video content, in response to the growing popularity of TikTok. Facebook has integrated shopping features that allow businesses to set up storefronts directly on the platform, reducing the friction between product discovery and purchase. LinkedIn has become a powerhouse for professional networking and B2B marketing, emphasizing content that fosters engagement and thought leadership.

These changes mean that businesses must stay agile and continually adapt their strategies to keep pace with platform innovations. What worked a year ago might not be as effective today, making it crucial for marketers to remain informed about the latest trends and updates.

- **The Rise of Influencer Marketing**

Influencer marketing has cemented its place as a pivotal strategy in the social media marketing playbook. Influencers, with their ability to sway consumer opinions and drive engagement, have become invaluable partners for brands looking to expand their reach authentically. From micro-influencers with niche, highly-engaged followings to macro-influencers and celebrities, the influencer ecosystem offers diverse opportunities for businesses of all sizes.

However, this landscape is also becoming more regulated. Transparency and authenticity are paramount, with platforms and governments alike enforcing stricter guidelines around sponsored content. Brands must navigate these regulations carefully, ensuring that their influencer partnerships are not only effective but also compliant and ethical.

- **Data Privacy and Ethical Considerations**

As social media platforms continue to amass vast amounts of user data, concerns around privacy and data protection have intensified. Scandals such as the Cambridge Analytica incident have led to increased scrutiny and stricter regulations, including the General Data Protection Regulation (GDPR) in Europe and the California Consumer Privacy Act (CCPA) in the United States.

For businesses, this means that data-driven marketing strategies must be executed with a heightened awareness of privacy laws and ethical considerations. Obtaining user consent, being transparent about data usage, and ensuring robust security measures are no longer optional—they are essential practices that safeguard consumer trust and legal compliance.

- **The Importance of Social Media for Businesses**

With over 4.5 billion people using social media worldwide, these platforms offer unparalleled opportunities for businesses to connect with their audience, build brand loyalty, and drive sales. Let's explore the multifaceted importance of social media for businesses in 2024.

- **Building Brand Awareness and Loyalty**

Social media provides a global stage for brands to showcase their identity, values, and offerings. Through consistent and strategic content, businesses can build strong brand awareness and cultivate a loyal community of followers. Each post, story, and interaction contributes to shaping the brand's narrative and forging a deeper connection with the audience.

Brand loyalty is further enhanced through active engagement. Responding to comments, participating in conversations, and addressing customer queries promptly fosters a sense of community and trust. This open channel of contact between companies and customers humanizes the brand and increases its approachability and relatability.

- **Driving Traffic and Conversions**

One of the most tangible benefits of social media marketing is its ability to drive traffic to a business's website and convert followers into customers. By strategically placing links, calls to action, and utilizing features like swipe-up links in Instagram Stories or shoppable posts, businesses can guide their social media audience along the buyer's journey seamlessly.

Moreover, the integration of e-commerce functionalities within social media platforms has streamlined the shopping experience. Features like Instagram Shopping, Facebook Shops, and Pinterest's Shop the Look allow users to discover and purchase products without leaving the app. This convenience significantly reduces the barriers to purchase, increasing the likelihood of conversions.

- **Enhancing Customer Insights**

Social media platforms offer a wealth of data and analytics that can provide deep insights into consumer behavior, preferences, and trends. By analyzing metrics such as engagement rates, reach, and audience demographics, businesses can fine-tune their marketing strategies to better meet the needs and desires of their target audience.

Tools like Facebook Insights, Instagram Analytics, and Twitter Analytics provide valuable information about what types of content resonate most with the audience, the best times to post, and how followers are interacting with the brand. These insights are instrumental in crafting content that not only engages but also drives meaningful results.

- **Cost-Effective Marketing**

Social media marketing is more affordable than traditional advertising methods. Businesses can reach a vast audience with a modest budget through targeted ads and organic content. The ability to precisely target ads based on user demographics, interests, and behaviors ensures that marketing dollars are spent efficiently, maximizing return on investment (ROI).

Furthermore, the rise of user-generated content (UGC) provides an additional avenue for cost-effective marketing. Encouraging customers to share their experiences and tag the brand can amplify reach and credibility without significant expenditure. UGC not only serves as authentic social proof but also fosters a deeper connection between the brand and its community.

- **Facilitating Real-Time Engagement**

In today's fast-paced digital world, real-time engagement is crucial. Social media platforms allow businesses to interact with their audience instantly, whether through comments, direct messages, or live streaming. This immediacy is invaluable for handling customer service inquiries, launching new products, and responding to market changes swiftly.

Live streaming, in particular, has gained immense popularity as a tool for real-time engagement. Platforms like Instagram Live, Facebook Live, and YouTube Live enable brands to host events, Q&A sessions, and product demonstrations, creating an interactive and immersive experience for viewers. This real-time interaction helps build a sense of urgency and excitement, driving higher engagement rates.

In conclusion, Social media marketing is crucial, and its significance cannot be emphasized as we move through 2024. The current landscape, characterized by rapid platform evolution, the prominence of influencer marketing, and heightened data privacy concerns, presents both challenges and opportunities for businesses.

By understanding these dynamics and leveraging the unique strengths of social media, businesses can build strong brand awareness, drive traffic and conversions, gain valuable customer insights, and engage with their audience in real-time. The subsequent chapters of this book will delve deeper into the strategies and tools that will empower you to harness the full potential of social media marketing, just as Jake did.

So, whether you are a seasoned marketer looking to refine your approach or a newcomer eager to make your mark, this guide will equip you with the knowledge and skills to prosper in the ever changing realm of social media marketing. Welcome to your journey towards digital marketing mastery.

Chapter 2

Setting Goals and Objectives

- **Defining Your Marketing Objectives**

Every successful marketing strategy starts with a clear vision of what you want to achieve. Setting well-defined marketing objectives is like plotting a course on a map; it guides your efforts and ensures you're heading in the right direction. Without these objectives, your social media activities can feel aimless, making it challenging to measure success or understand where to improve.

- **The Importance of Clear Objectives**

Imagine you're on a journey without a destination in mind. You might take a few scenic routes, but you'll likely end up lost, frustrated, and far from where you intended. The same goes for social media marketing. Clear objectives provide focus, aligning your efforts with your broader business goals. They help you stay on track, allocate resources effectively, and evaluate your progress.

Clear objectives also serve as a motivational tool for your team. When everyone understands the goals, they can work cohesively towards them, knowing what success looks like and how their contributions matter.

- **How to Define Your Objectives**

1. Start with Your Business Goals: Your social media objectives should directly support your overarching business goals. Whether you aim to increase brand awareness, drive sales, or build customer loyalty, aligning your social media efforts with these goals ensures consistency and coherence in your strategy.

2. Be Specific: Vague goals like "increase followers" or "boost engagement" are a starting point but lack the precision needed for effective planning. Specify what you mean by "increase" or "boost." For instance, aim to "increase Instagram followers by 25% in the next six months" or "achieve a 10% engagement rate on Facebook posts by the end of the quarter."

3. Ensure Measurability: To track your progress, your objectives must be measurable. This involves defining metrics that can quantify your success. For example, if your goal is to drive website traffic, set a target for the number of clicks from social media posts to your site.

4. Set Achievable Goals: While ambition is good, setting unrealistic objectives can lead to frustration and demotivation. Ensure your goals are attainable with the resources, time, and budget available to you. It's better to achieve a series of smaller, incremental goals than to fall short of a grandiose target.

5. Relevance to Your Brand: Your objectives should align with your brand's mission and values. They should reflect what your brand stands for and how you want to be perceived by your audience. For example, if you're a sustainable fashion brand, an objective might be to increase awareness of your eco-friendly practices.

6. Time-Bound: Setting a deadline for your objectives creates a sense of urgency and helps prioritize tasks. Whether it's a quarterly goal or a year-long target, having a timeframe ensures you maintain momentum and can evaluate progress at regular intervals.

- **Establishing Key Performance Indicators (KPIs)**

Once you have your objectives in place, the next step is to determine how you will measure success. This is where KPIs, or key performance indicators, are useful. KPIs are specific metrics that provide insights into your performance relative to your objectives. They act as signposts, guiding you towards your goals and highlighting areas that need adjustment.

KPIs offer a tangible way to track your progress and determine the effectiveness of your social media strategies. They help you understand what's working, what isn't, and where you need to pivot. By regularly monitoring KPIs, you can make data-driven decisions that optimize your efforts and maximize your return on investment (ROI).

- **Selecting the Right KPIs**

Choosing the right KPIs depends on your specific objectives. Here are some common KPIs aligned with different types of social media goals:

1. Increasing Brand Awareness:
   - **Reach:** The number of unique users who have seen your content.
   - Impression: The total number of times your content is displayed, regardless of whether it's clicked.
   - **Follower Growth Rate:** The percentage increase in followers over a specific period.

2. Driving Engagement:
   - **Engagement Rate:** The ratio of engagements (likes, comments, shares) to total followers.

- **Click-Through Rate (CTR):** This is the proportion of readers who click on a post's link.
- Average Engagement per Post: The total engagement divided by the number of posts.

3. Generating Leads and Sales:
- **Conversion Rate:** The percentage of users who complete a desired action, such as filling out a form or making a purchase.
- **Lead Generation:** The number of new leads acquired through social media.
- **Sales Revenue:** The total revenue generated from social media campaigns.

4. Improving Customer Service:
- **Response Time:** The typical amount of time needed to address questions from clients.
- **Customer Satisfaction (CSAT) Score:** A measure of how satisfied

customers are with your social media interactions.

-**Resolution Rate:** The percentage of customer issues resolved through social media.

- **Implementing and Tracking KPIs**

1. Tools and Platforms: Utilize analytics tools provided by social media platforms, such as Facebook Insights, Instagram Analytics, and Twitter Analytics. Additionally, third-party tools like Hootsuite, Sprout Social, and Google Analytics offer comprehensive tracking capabilities.

2. Regular Monitoring: Establish a routine for reviewing your KPIs. This could be weekly, monthly, or quarterly, depending on your campaign's duration and intensity. Regular monitoring allows you to identify trends, spot potential issues early, and make timely adjustments.

3. Benchmarking: Compare your KPIs against industry standards or past performance to gauge how well you're doing. This context helps you understand whether your metrics are strong, average, or need improvement.

4. Adjusting Strategies: Use the insights gained from your KPIs to refine your strategies. If a particular type of content isn't performing well, experiment with different formats or topics. If engagement is low, consider more interactive posts like polls, Q&A sessions, or live videos.

5. Reporting and Communication: Share your KPI reports with your team to keep everyone aligned and informed. Transparent communication about what's working and what needs adjustment fosters a collaborative environment where everyone is focused on the same goals.

In conclusion, Setting clear goals and objectives, along with establishing the right KPIs, forms the foundation of a successful social media marketing strategy. These elements guide your efforts, provide direction, and enable you to measure your progress effectively. By understanding what you want to achieve and how you will measure success, you can navigate the complex landscape of social media with confidence and purpose.

As you proceed, keep in mind that adaptability and flexibility are essential. The social media environment is ever-changing, and what works today might need adjustment tomorrow. Stay informed, be willing to pivot, and continuously refine your strategies based on the insights gained from your KPIs.

In the subsequent chapters, we'll delve deeper into specific strategies and tools that will help you achieve your objectives, engage your audience, and grow your brand on social media. With a solid foundation in goal-setting and performance measurement, you're well on your way to mastering social media marketing and driving significant results for your business.

Chapter 3

Target Audience Identification

- **Identifying Your Ideal Customer**

In the realm of social media marketing, there isn't one strategy that works for everyone. Understanding and identifying your ideal customer is pivotal to crafting messages that resonate, creating products that fulfill their needs, and ultimately, achieving your marketing objectives. This chapter will guide you through the process of identifying and understanding your target audience in a detailed and actionable manner.

- **The Significance of Knowing Your Audience**

Imagine trying to sell winter coats in a tropical climate or promoting high-end luxury items to budget-conscious students. Without a clear understanding of who your ideal customer is, your marketing efforts can miss the mark entirely, wasting valuable time and resources. Knowing your audience allows you to tailor your content, messaging, and products to meet their specific needs and preferences, resulting in higher engagement, better customer relationships, and increased sales.

- **Steps to Identify Your Ideal Customer**

1. Market Research: Begin with comprehensive market research to gather data about your potential customers. This involves understanding the market demand, identifying industry trends, and analyzing your competitors. Tools like surveys, questionnaires, and market reports can provide valuable insights.

2. Demographic Analysis: Identify the key demographic characteristics of your ideal customer. These consist of geographic location, age, gender, economic bracket, occupation, and education. Demographic information helps in crafting messages that resonate with specific segments of your audience. For example, a skincare brand targeting young adults will use different language and imagery compared to one targeting mature audiences.

3. Psychographic Profiling: Delve deeper into the psychographics of your audience. This involves understanding their interests, values, lifestyles, and behaviors. Psychographic profiling gives you a more nuanced view of your customers, allowing you to create highly personalized marketing campaigns. For instance, a brand targeting health-conscious consumers might focus on promoting the organic and sustainable aspects of their products.

4. Behavioral Analysis: Analyze the online behavior of your target audience. This includes their purchasing habits, social media usage patterns, preferred platforms, and engagement levels. Understanding how your audience interacts with social media helps in choosing the right platforms and crafting content that encourages interaction and engagement.

5. Customer Feedback and Insights: Leverage feedback from your existing customers to gain insights into what they value and what they expect from your brand. Reviews, testimonials, and direct feedback can reveal common pain points and areas for improvement. Engaging with your audience through surveys and direct messages can also provide firsthand insights into their preferences and expectations.

6. Creating Buyer Personas: Consolidate the data gathered from the above steps into detailed buyer personas. Based on actual data and insights, a buyer persona is a semi-fictionalized depiction of your ideal client. Each persona should include demographic information, psychographic details, behavioral traits, and specific pain points. Creating multiple personas can help address the diverse segments within your target audience.

- **Utilizing Audience Insights for Targeting**

Once you have identified your ideal customer, the next step is to leverage these insights for precise targeting. Social media platforms offer robust tools and analytics that can help you reach your audience effectively. Here's how to utilize audience insights for optimal targeting.

- **Leveraging Social Media Analytics**

1. Platform-Specific Insights: Each social media platform provides its own set of analytics tools that offer deep insights into your audience. For example, Facebook Audience Insights, Instagram Insights, Twitter Analytics, and LinkedIn Analytics can provide detailed information about your followers, including their demographics, interests, and engagement patterns. Use these tools to refine your targeting and understand which content resonates most with your audience.

2. Engagement Metrics: Monitor engagement metrics such as likes, comments, shares, and click-through rates to gauge which types of content your audience prefers. High engagement rates on certain posts indicate that the content is resonating well with your audience. With this knowledge, produce more of the content that appeals to your audience and less of the stuff that doesn't.

3. Audience Growth: Track the growth of your audience over time. Understanding how and when your audience grows can provide insights into the effectiveness of your campaigns. If you notice a spike in followers after a specific campaign, analyze what worked and consider replicating similar strategies in future campaigns.

- **Utilizing Targeting Features on Social Media Platforms**

1. Custom Audiences: You may make custom audiences on social media sites like Facebook and Instagram by defining certain parameters. You can upload your customer list, use website visitor data, or create lookalike audiences that match the characteristics of your best customers. Custom audiences enable highly targeted campaigns, increasing the likelihood of reaching individuals who are interested in your offerings.

2. Interest and Behavior Targeting: Use interest and behavior targeting to reach users based on their activities, interests, and behaviors. For instance, if you're a fitness brand, you can target users who follow fitness influencers, engage with fitness-related content, or have purchased fitness products in the past. This level of targeting ensures your ads are shown to users who are more likely to engage with your brand.

3. Geotargeting: Geotargeting allows you to reach audiences based on their geographic location. This is particularly useful for local businesses or brands with location-specific offers.

For example, a restaurant can target ads to users within a certain radius, or an e-commerce store can promote special deals to users in specific regions.

- **Crafting Tailored Content**

1. Personalized Messaging: Use the insights gained from your audience analysis to craft personalized messages that speak directly to the needs and desires of your audience. Personalized content is more likely to capture attention and drive engagement. For example, if your audience values sustainability, highlight the eco-friendly aspects of your products in your messaging.

2. Content Formats: Different segments of your audience might prefer different types of content. Some might engage more with videos, while others prefer blog posts or infographics. Use your audience insights to determine the preferred content formats and create a diverse content mix that caters to these preferences.

3. Timing and Frequency: Understanding when your audience is most active on social media can help in scheduling your posts for maximum visibility and engagement. Use analytics tools to identify peak engagement times and plan your content calendar accordingly. Additionally, maintaining an optimal posting frequency ensures that your audience stays engaged without feeling overwhelmed.

In conclusion, Identifying your target audience and utilizing audience insights for targeting are crucial steps in developing an effective social media marketing strategy. By deeply understanding who your ideal customers are, what they value, and how they behave online, you can create targeted and personalized marketing campaigns that resonate with your audience and drive meaningful results.

The process of identifying your audience is not a one-time task but an ongoing effort. Continuously gather data, analyze trends, and refine your personas to stay aligned with the evolving preferences and behaviors of your audience. The subsequent chapters of this book will delve into specific tactics and tools that will help you further refine your targeting and engagement strategies.

By putting your audience at the heart of your social media marketing efforts, you can build stronger connections, foster brand loyalty, and achieve your business objectives more effectively. As you move forward, remember that the insights gained from your audience are not just data points but valuable guidance that shapes your entire marketing approach.

Chapter 4

Platform Selection and Optimization

- **Choosing the Right Social Media Platforms**

In the vast world of social media, not all platforms are created equal. Each platform offers unique features, audiences, and opportunities for engagement. The key to successful social media marketing lies in choosing the right platforms for your business and optimizing your presence on them. This chapter will guide you through the process of selecting the most suitable platforms and maximizing their potential for your brand.

- **The Importance of Platform Selection**

Imagine trying to sell a luxury car in a marketplace where everyone is looking for budget-friendly options. No matter how compelling your message is, it won't resonate because the audience isn't right. Similarly, choosing the wrong social media platforms can result in wasted efforts and resources. The right platform ensures that your message reaches the audience most likely to engage with and benefit from your offerings.

- **Evaluating Platform Demographics and Features**

To choose the right platforms, start by understanding the demographics and features of each. The following are some of the most well-known social networking sites and the services they provide:

1. Facebook:
   - Demographics: With over 2.8 billion monthly active users, Facebook

has a diverse user base spanning various age groups, but it's particularly popular among users aged 25-54.
- Features: Facebook offers robust advertising options, groups, pages, events, and a variety of content formats (posts, videos, stories).
- Best For: Building community, detailed targeting, and versatile content sharing.

2. Instagram:
- Demographics: Instagram has over 1 billion monthly active users, predominantly younger audiences (18-34 years old).
- Features: Visual-centric platform with posts, stories, IGTV, Reels, and shopping features.
- Best For: Visual storytelling, influencer marketing, and brand aesthetics.

3. Twitter:
- Demographics: Twitter has approximately 330 million monthly active users, with a strong presence among 18-49-year-olds.
- Features: Real-time updates, trending topics, threads, and engagement with hashtags.
- Best For: Real-time engagement, customer service, and trending conversations.

4. LinkedIn:
- Demographics: LinkedIn has over 774 million users, primarily professionals and B2B audiences.
- Features: Professional networking, company pages, articles, and job postings.
- Best For: B2B marketing, professional branding, and thought leadership.

5. TikTok:
- Demographics: TikTok has around 1 billion monthly active users, predominantly younger audiences (16-24 years old).
- Features: Short-form video content, trending challenges, and music integration.
- Best For: Viral content, engaging younger audiences, and creative marketing.

6. Pinterest:
- Demographics: Pinterest has over 400 million monthly active users, with a strong female demographic (60%).
- Features: Visual discovery, pinboards, and shopping integration.
- Best For: Lifestyle, DIY, fashion, and home décor content.

- **Matching Platforms to Your Audience and Goals**

Once you understand the demographics and features of each

platform, match them to your target audience and marketing goals. Here's how to approach this:

1. Identify Where Your Audience Spends Their Time:
- Use market research and analytics tools to find out which platforms your target audience prefers. For example, TikTok and Instagram might work better if your target audience is primarily young adults.

2. Align Platform Strengths with Your Objectives:
- Determine which platforms best support your marketing objectives. If your goal is to drive website traffic, platforms with strong link-sharing capabilities like Facebook and Twitter are ideal. For brand awareness and visual engagement, Instagram and Pinterest may be more suitable.

3. Consider Content Format Preferences:
- Different platforms favor different content formats. If your brand excels in creating high-quality videos, YouTube and TikTok are great choices. For long-form content, LinkedIn and Facebook are more appropriate.

- **Optimizing Profiles for Maximum Impact**

Having chosen the right platforms, the next step is to optimize your profiles for maximum impact. A well-optimized profile not only attracts followers but also encourages engagement and builds trust. Here's a comprehensive guide to optimizing your social media profiles.

- **Consistent Branding Across Platforms**

Consistency in branding is crucial to creating a cohesive and recognizable presence across multiple platforms. Here's how to maintain consistency:

1. Profile and Cover Photos:
- Use the same profile picture (typically your logo) and cover photo across all platforms to ensure brand recognition. The cover photo should reflect your brand's current campaigns or values.

2. Bio and Descriptions:
- Craft a compelling and concise bio that communicates your brand's mission, values, and what followers can expect. Use similar wording across platforms but tailor it to the specific audience and character limits of each platform.

3. Username and Handles:
- Ensure your username and handles are consistent across all platforms. This makes it easier for users to find and tag you.

- **Enhancing Profile Information**

1. Contact Information:
- Include accurate and up-to-date contact information such as email, phone number, and physical address if applicable. Ensure it's easy for users to reach you.

2. Website Links:
- Add links to your website, blog, or specific landing pages. Use link-in-bio tools like Linktree for Instagram to direct users to multiple destinations.

3. Call to Action (CTA):
- Incorporate a clear CTA in your bio, such as "Shop Now," "Sign Up," or "Contact Us." This directs users to take immediate action and engage with your brand further.

- **Content Strategy and Posting Schedule**

1. Content Calendar:

- Create a content calendar to schedule your posts ahead of time. This ensures a steady flow of content and helps you maintain consistency. Consider using scheduling tools like Hootsuite or Buffer to automate posts.

2. Content Mix:
- Diversify your content mix to include a variety of posts such as educational content, promotional offers, user-generated content, and behind-the-scenes glimpses. This keeps your feed interesting and engaging.

3. Optimal Posting Times:
- Examine the behavior of your audience to ascertain the ideal posting times. Most platforms provide analytics that show when your followers are most active. Posting at these times increases the likelihood of engagement.

Engaging with Your Audience
Responding to Comments and Messages:
Promptly respond to comments and direct messages. Interacting with your audience creates a sense of community and trust. Recognise compliments, and handle complaints or issues with professionalism.

Interactive Content:
Use interactive content such as polls, quizzes, and Q&A sessions to engage your audience. Features like Instagram Stories and Facebook Live offer excellent opportunities for real-time interaction.

Community Building:
Participate in relevant groups and forums to build a community around your brand. On platforms like Facebook and LinkedIn, creating or joining groups related to your industry can position you as a thought leader

and foster deeper connections with your audience.

Monitoring and Analyzing Performance

Analytics Tools:
Use platform-specific analytics tools to monitor the performance of your posts and overall profile. Keep an eye on important data like follower growth, impressions, reach, and engagement rate.

Regular Audits:
Conduct regular audits of your social media profiles to identify areas for improvement. Look at your top-performing content and analyze why it resonated with your audience. Similarly, identify underperforming content and adjust your strategy accordingly.

Adapting Strategies:
Be flexible and ready to adapt your strategies based on your analytics. If you notice that a particular type of content or posting time is performing exceptionally well, incorporate those insights into your future planning.

In conclusion, Choosing the right social media platforms and optimizing your profiles are foundational steps in building a strong and effective social media presence. By understanding the demographics and features of each platform, aligning them with your audience and goals, and optimizing your profiles for maximum impact, you can create a cohesive and engaging social media strategy.

Remember, the social media landscape is dynamic, and staying updated with the latest trends and platform features is essential. Regularly review your platform selection and profile optimizations to ensure they remain aligned with your evolving business goals and audience preferences.

In the following chapters, we will explore content creation, advertising strategies, and advanced analytics to further enhance your social media marketing efforts. With a solid foundation in platform selection and optimization, you are well on your way to building a powerful and effective social media presence that drives meaningful results for your business.

Chapter 5

Content Strategy and Creation

- **Crafting Engaging Content**

The foundation of every effective social media strategy is content. It's what captures the attention of your audience, communicates your brand's message, and drives engagement. Crafting engaging content requires a deep understanding of your audience, creativity, and a strategic approach. This chapter will guide you through developing a content strategy that resonates with your audience and drives meaningful engagement.

- **Understanding Your Audience**

Before you start creating content, it's crucial to have a clear understanding of your target audience. This involves knowing their interests, preferences, pain points, and the type of content they are likely to engage with. Use the audience insights you've gathered to tailor your content to their needs and preferences.

1. Personas: Refer back to the detailed buyer personas you created. These personas should guide your content creation process, ensuring that each piece of content speaks directly to the needs and interests of your audience segments.

2. Engagement Patterns: Analyze past performance data to understand what types of content your audience engages with the most. Look at metrics like likes, shares, comments, and views to identify trends and preferences.

- **Setting Content Goals**

Your content strategy should align with your broader marketing objectives. Whether your goal is to increase brand awareness, drive traffic to your website, generate leads, or boost sales, your content should be designed to support these goals.

1. SMART Goals: Set SMART (Specific, Measurable, Achievable, Relevant, Time-bound) goals for your content strategy. For example, a SMART goal might be to increase website traffic from social media by 20% over the next three months.

2. Content Pillars: Define your content pillars, which are the main themes or topics that your content will focus on. These pillars should be aligned with your brand's mission and resonate with your audience. For instance, a health and wellness brand might have content pillars such as nutrition tips, fitness routines, mental health, and product highlights.

- **Developing a Content Calendar**

A content calendar helps you plan and organize your content in advance, ensuring a consistent and strategic approach. It allows you to balance different types of content and schedule posts at optimal times.

1. Frequency and Timing: Determine how often you will post on each platform. Use analytics to identify the best times to post for maximum engagement. Consistency is key, but quality should never be sacrificed for quantity.

2. Variety and Balance: Ensure a good mix of content types, including promotional posts, educational content, entertaining posts, and user-generated content. This keeps your feed diverse and engaging.

3. Seasonal and Topical Content: Incorporate seasonal themes, holidays, and trending topics into your content calendar. This makes your content timely and relevant, increasing the likelihood of engagement.

- **Incorporating Visuals and Multimedia**

In the visually-driven world of social media, incorporating high-quality visuals and multimedia is essential. Visual content not only grabs attention but also enhances your message and improves engagement.

Visual content is processed faster by the human brain and is more likely to be remembered than text. It can evoke emotions, tell stories, and convey complex information quickly. Here's how to effectively incorporate visuals into your content strategy:

1. Images: Use high-quality, relevant images that complement your message. Stock photos can be useful, but original images tend to perform better as they are more authentic and unique to your brand.

2. Infographics: Infographics are great for presenting data and information in a visually appealing and easily digestible format. They can simplify complex concepts and make them more engaging.

3. Videos: Video content is incredibly powerful for storytelling and engagement. It allows you to showcase your products, share behind-the-scenes glimpses, conduct interviews, and more. Use a mix of short-form videos (like those on TikTok and Instagram Reels) and long-form videos (such as those on YouTube and IGTV).

4. GIFs and Memes: These are perfect for adding humor and personality to your content. They can make your brand more relatable and increase shares and engagement.

- **Creating High-Quality Visuals**

1. Consistency in Branding: Ensure that all visual content aligns with your brand's visual identity. This includes using a consistent color palette, fonts, and style. Consistency helps in building a recognizable and cohesive brand presence.

2. Professional Tools: Use professional tools and software for creating and editing visuals. Tools like Adobe Photoshop, Illustrator, Canva, and Lightroom can help you produce high-quality images and graphics.

3. User-Generated Content: Encourage your audience to create and share content featuring your brand. User-generated content not only provides you with authentic visuals but also builds community and trust. Always give credit to the creators when sharing their content.

- **Optimizing Multimedia for Different Platforms**

Each social media platform has its own specifications and best practices for visual content. Here's how to optimize your visuals for maximum impact on different platforms:

1. Facebook: Use a mix of images, videos, and infographics. Square images (1080x1080 pixels) and horizontal videos (1280x720 pixels) work best. Facebook Live videos are also effective for real-time engagement.

2. Instagram: Focus on high-quality images and short videos. Use

Instagram Stories, Reels, and IGTV for diverse content formats. Vertical images (1080 x 1350 pixels) and videos (1080x1920 pixels) perform well on Instagram.

3. Twitter: Use images and GIFs to stand out in the fast-paced Twitter feed. Optimal image size is 1200x675 pixels. Videos should be under 2 minutes and 20 seconds for better engagement.

4. LinkedIn: Use professional and informative visuals. Images (1200x627 pixels) and videos (horizontal, 1280x720 pixels) should be polished and aligned with your brand's professional tone.

5. Pinterest: Focus on vertical images and infographics. Ideal image size is 1000x1500 pixels. High-quality, visually appealing pins with detailed descriptions perform best.

6. TikTok: Short-form vertical videos (1080x1920 pixels) are the key. Use trending music, hashtags, and challenges to increase visibility and engagement.

- **Leveraging Interactive Content**

Interactive content increases engagement by encouraging users to participate. Here are some ways to incorporate interactivity into your content strategy:

Polls and Quizzes: Use polls and quizzes on platforms like Instagram Stories, Facebook, and Twitter to engage your audience. They are fun, easy to participate in, and provide valuable insights into your audience's preferences.

Contests and Giveaways: Run contests and giveaways to encourage user participation and generate excitement around your brand. Ask users to share your content, tag friends, or create their own content to enter.

Live Streaming: Live streaming on platforms like Facebook, Instagram, and YouTube allows for real-time interaction with your audience. Use live streams for product launches, Q&A sessions, behind-the-scenes tours, and more.

Augmented Reality (AR) Filters: Create branded AR filters for platforms like Instagram and Snapchat. These fun and interactive filters can increase brand awareness and engagement.

In conclusion, Crafting engaging content and incorporating visuals and multimedia are essential components of a successful social media strategy. By understanding your audience, setting clear content goals, and developing a well-planned content calendar, you can create content that resonates and drives engagement.

High-quality visuals and multimedia enhance your content's appeal and effectiveness. Ensure consistency in branding, use professional tools, and optimize your visuals for each platform's specifications. Interactive content further boosts engagement by encouraging active participation from your audience.

In the next chapters, we will explore advertising strategies, community management, and advanced analytics to further refine your social media marketing efforts. With a solid content strategy and the right visuals, you're well on your way to creating a compelling and effective social media presence that captivates your audience and achieves your business objectives.

Chapter 6

Community Engagement and Management

- **Building Relationships with Your Audience**

Social media marketing is centered on community interaction. It's not enough to simply post content and hope for the best; true success comes from actively building and nurturing relationships with your audience. In this chapter, we'll explore the strategies and practices that will help you connect with your community on a deeper level, turning followers into loyal advocates.

- **The Importance of Authenticity**

In a digital world flooded with content, authenticity stands out. People crave genuine interactions and are quick to recognize (and dismiss) inauthenticity. Here's how to ensure your engagement efforts feel real and meaningful:

1. Be Human: Show the human side of your brand. Share behind-the-scenes content, introduce your team, and let your personality shine through. Respond to comments and messages in a personable and friendly manner.

2. Transparency: Be open and honest with your audience. If there's an issue, address it head-on rather than trying to cover it up. Transparency builds trust, which is essential for long-term engagement.

3. Consistency: Regular and consistent engagement is key. Make it a habit to interact with your audience daily, whether through responding to comments, participating in discussions, or acknowledging user-generated content.

- **Strategies for Building Relationships**

1. Active Listening: Pay attention to what your audience is saying. Use social listening tools to monitor conversations about your brand, industry, and competitors. This helps you understand your audience's needs and interests, allowing you to engage in meaningful ways.

2. Two-Way Conversations: Engagement is a two-way street. Don't just broadcast messages; encourage conversations. Ask questions, seek opinions, and show that you value your audience's input.

3. Personalization: Tailor your interactions to the individual. Use their names, reference previous interactions, and make them feel seen and heard. Personalized engagement fosters deeper connections.

4. User-Generated Content (UGC): Encourage your audience to create content featuring your brand. Highlight and share this content to show appreciation and build a sense of community. Not only can user-generated content increase engagement, but it also acts as genuine endorsements for your brand.

5. Exclusive Content and Offers: Reward your loyal followers with exclusive content, early access to products, or special offers. This not only incentivizes engagement but also makes your audience feel valued and appreciated.

- **Handling Customer Inquiries and Feedback**

Social media is often the first place customers go to ask questions, seek support, or give feedback. How you handle these interactions can significantly impact your brand's reputation and customer satisfaction. Here's how to manage customer inquiries and feedback effectively:

Timely and Efficient Responses

1. Set Expectations: Clearly communicate your response times in your bio or pinned posts. For example, "We typically respond within 24 hours." This sets expectations and reduces frustration.

2. Prioritize Urgency: Triage inquiries based on urgency. Address urgent or negative feedback quickly to prevent escalation. Use customer service management tools to streamline this process.

3. Automated Responses: Use automated responses for common inquiries. Chatbots can handle simple questions, provide quick answers, and direct users to relevant resources. However, always ensure there's an option to speak to a human for more complex issues.

- **Providing Helpful and Accurate Information**

1. Knowledgeable Support: Ensure your social media team is well-trained and knowledgeable about your products, services, and policies. They ought to have quick access to accurate and beneficial information.

2. Resource Library: Create a resource library with FAQs, tutorials, and troubleshooting guides. This can help address common inquiries efficiently and empower your audience to find answers on their own.

3. Escalation Protocols: Establish clear protocols for escalating issues that cannot be resolved on social media. This ensures that more complex problems are handled appropriately by the right teams.

- **Handling Negative Feedback**

Negative feedback is inevitable, but how you handle it can turn a dissatisfied customer into a loyal advocate. Here's how to approach it:

1. Stay Calm and Professional: Never respond to negative feedback with anger or defensiveness. Remain calm, professional, and empathetic.

2. Acknowledge and Apologize: Acknowledge the issue and apologize if necessary. Even if the problem wasn't your fault, a simple apology can go a long way in diffusing tension.

3. Take It Offline: For complex or sensitive issues, invite the customer to continue the conversation privately through direct messages, email, or phone. This prevents the situation from escalating publicly and allows for a more detailed resolution.

4. Follow Up: After the problem has been fixed, get in touch with the client to make sure they are happy with the solution. This demonstrates your sincere concern for their situation and your resolve to put things right.

- **Encouraging Positive Feedback**
-

1. Ask for Reviews: Encourage satisfied customers to leave reviews or testimonials. Highlight these positive experiences on your social media channels to build credibility and attract new followers.

2. Show Appreciation: Publicly thank customers for positive feedback. A simple "Thank you for your kind words!" goes a long way towards encouraging kindness and expressing thanks.

3. Incorporate Feedback: Use positive feedback to identify what's working well and share it with your team. This can help reinforce successful practices and inspire continuous improvement.

- **Building a Loyal Community**

A loyal community not only engages with your content but also advocates for your brand. Here's how to cultivate loyalty within your social media community:

- **Recognize and Reward Loyalty**

1. Engagement Programs: Create engagement programs or loyalty clubs that offer exclusive perks to active community members. This can include early access to new products, special discounts, or members-only content.

2. Spotlight Your Followers: Regularly feature your most engaged followers in your posts or stories. Other people may get more involved as a result of this acknowledgment.

3. Host Events: Organize virtual or in-person events for your community. Webinars, live Q&A sessions, and meetups can strengthen the sense of belonging and foster deeper connections.

- **Foster a Sense of Belonging**

Inclusive Community: Ensure your community feels inclusive and welcoming to all. Celebrate diversity and create a safe space where everyone feels valued and respected.

Shared Values: Communicate your brand's values clearly and consistently. When your community shares these values, it strengthens their connection to your brand.

Meaningful Interactions: Go beyond surface-level interactions. Engage in meaningful conversations, ask thought-provoking questions, and show genuine interest in your community's opinions and experiences.

In conclusion, Community engagement and management are vital components of a successful social media strategy. By building authentic relationships, providing timely and helpful support, and fostering a loyal community, you can turn your social media channels into thriving hubs of interaction and advocacy.

Remember, engagement is not just about numbers; it's about building genuine connections and creating a positive experience for your audience. In the next chapters, we will delve into advertising strategies, advanced analytics, and the future of social media marketing. With a strong foundation in community engagement, you're well-equipped to take your social media presence to the next level and achieve lasting success.

Chapter 7

Paid Advertising and Promotion

- **Understanding Paid Advertising Options**

In the crowded landscape of social media, organic reach alone is often insufficient to achieve your marketing goals. Paid advertising provides a powerful means to amplify your message, reach a broader audience, and drive specific actions such as clicks, conversions, and sales. In this chapter, we'll explore the various paid advertising options available on major social media platforms and how to create effective ad campaigns that deliver results.

- **The Spectrum of Paid Advertising**

Each social media platform offers unique advertising options tailored to different goals and audiences. Here's an overview of the primary advertising options available on popular platforms:

1. Facebook Ads:

   - **Ad Types:** Facebook offers a wide range of ad formats including image ads, video ads, carousel ads, slideshow ads, and collection ads.

   - **Placement Options:** Ads can appear in the News Feed, Stories, Marketplace, video feeds, and more.

   - **Targeting Capability:** Facebook's sophisticated targeting options allow you to reach specific demographics, interests, behaviors, and custom audiences.

2. Instagram Ads:
- **Ad Types:** Instagram ads include photo ads, video ads, carousel ads, and Stories ads.
- **Visual Focus:** Given Instagram's visual-centric nature, high-quality, eye-catching visuals are crucial.
- **Integration with Facebook:** Instagram ads are managed through Facebook's Ad Manager, offering similar targeting options.

3. Twitter Ads:
- **Ad Type:** Twitter offers promoted tweets, promoted accounts, and promoted trends.
- **Real-Time Engagement:** Twitter's real-time nature makes it ideal for promoting time-sensitive content or participating in trending conversations.

4. LinkedIn Ads:
- **Ad Types:** LinkedIn provides sponsored content, sponsored InMail, text ads, and dynamic ads.

- **Professional Audience:** LinkedIn is particularly effective for B2B marketing, allowing you to target professionals based on job title, industry, and company size.

5. YouTube Ads:
- **Ad Types:** YouTube ads include skippable and non-skippable video ads, bumper ads, overlay ads, and sponsored cards.
- **Video Focus:** Given YouTube's platform, high-quality video content is essential for effective advertising.

6. Pinterest Ads:
- **Ad Types:** Pinterest offers promoted pins, promoted video pins, and shopping ads.
- **Discovery-Based:** Pinterest's discovery-driven platform makes it ideal for promoting visually appealing products and content.

7. TikTok Ads:

- **Ad Type:** TikTok ads include in-feed ads, branded hashtags, brand takeovers, and branded effects.

- **Creative Engagement:** TikTok's emphasis on creative and entertaining content requires a unique approach to ad creation.

- **Creating Effective Ad Campaigns**

Creating an effective ad campaign involves a strategic approach that includes setting clear objectives, understanding your audience, designing compelling creatives, and continuously optimizing performance. Here's a step-by-step guide to developing successful social media ad campaigns:

1. Setting Clear Objectives

Your ad campaign should begin with clear, measurable objectives. These objectives will guide your campaign strategy and help you evaluate success. Common objectives include:

- **Brand Awareness:** Making your brand more noticeable and recognisable.
- **Traffic:** Driving visitors to your website or landing page.
-**Engagement:** Motivating people to interact with your content by leaving likes, comments, and shares.
- **Lead Generation:** Gathering data from prospective clients.
- **Conversions:** Driving specific actions such as purchases, sign-ups, or downloads.

2. Understanding Your Audience

To create effective ads, you need a deep understanding of your target audience. This involves:

- **Audience Research:** Use analytics and social listening tools to gather insights about your audience's demographics, interests, and behaviors.

- **Segmenting Your Audience:** Divide your audience into segments based on specific criteria such as age, location, interests, or buying behavior. This allows for more personalized and targeted ads.

- **Creating Buyer Personas:** Develop detailed buyer personas to represent different segments of your audience. These personas help in crafting messages that resonate with each group.

3. Designing Compelling Creatives

The creative elements of your ad are crucial for capturing attention and driving engagement. Effective ad creatives include:

- Visual Appeal: Use high-quality images and videos that are visually striking and relevant to your message.

Ensure that visuals are optimized for each platform's specifications.

- **Clear Messaging:** Your ad copy should be concise, clear, and compelling. Emphasize the salient features of your offering and incorporate a compelling call to action (CTA).

- **Consistency:** Maintain consistency with your brand's visual identity and tone of voice across all ads. This helps in building brand recognition and trust.

4. Optimizing Ad Placement and Budget

Optimizing your ad placement and budget ensures that your ads reach the right people at the right time without overspending. Consider the following:

- **Ad Placement:** Choose placements that align with your campaign objectives. For example, Stories ads might be more effective for engagement, while News Feed ads could drive more traffic.

- **Budget Allocation:** Determine your budget and allocate it based on the performance of different ad sets and placements. Use A/B testing to identify the most effective strategies.

- **Bidding Strategy:** Select a bidding strategy that aligns with your goals, whether it's cost-per-click (CPC), cost-per-impression (CPM), or cost-per-action (CPA).

5. Tracking and Analyzing Performance

Continuous tracking and analysis are essential for optimizing your ad campaigns. Use the following strategies:

- **Key Metrics:** Monitor key performance indicators (KPIs) such as click-through rates (CTR), conversion rates, return on ad spend (ROAS), and cost per conversion.

- **A/B Testing:** Conduct A/B tests to compare different ad creatives, headlines, CTAs, and targeting options. Refine your campaigns with the knowledge you've gathered.
- **Analytics Tools:** Utilize analytics tools provided by social media platforms, as well as third-party tools, to gain deeper insights into your ad performance.

6. Adjusting and Scaling Campaigns
Based on your analysis, make necessary adjustments to improve your campaign's performance. This may involve:

- **Refining Targeting:** Narrow down or expand your audience segments based on performance data.
- **Optimizing Creatives:** Update or replace underperforming creatives with new designs or copy.
- **Adjusting Budgets:** Reallocate budgets towards higher-performing ads

and reduce spending on less effective ones.
- **Scaling Successful Campaigns:** Once you identify successful ad sets, consider scaling them by increasing the budget or expanding the target audience.

- **Case Studies and Best Practices**
Examining case studies and best practices can provide valuable insights and inspiration for your own ad campaigns. Here are a few examples:

Brand Awareness Campaign: A fashion brand used Instagram Stories ads to showcase its new collection. By leveraging visually stunning images and a strong CTA to "Swipe Up" for more details, the campaign achieved a 30% increase in brand recall and a significant boost in website traffic.

Lead Generation Campaign: A software company ran LinkedIn sponsored content ads targeting professionals in specific industries. The ads featured a free e-book download in exchange for contact information. The campaign generated over 500 high-quality leads within a month.

Conversion Campaign: An e-commerce store utilized Facebook carousel ads to display a variety of products. Each image linked directly to the product page, accompanied by limited-time discount offers. The campaign saw a 20% increase in sales and a high ROAS.

In conclusion, Paid advertising on social media is a powerful tool for amplifying your reach, driving targeted actions, and achieving your marketing objectives. By understanding the various advertising options, setting clear goals, designing compelling creatives, and continuously optimizing performance, you can create effective ad campaigns that deliver tangible results.

Remember, the key to success lies in a strategic and data-driven approach. Stay informed about the latest trends and best practices, experiment with different strategies, and adapt to the ever-evolving social media landscape. In the next chapter, we'll delve into advanced analytics and measurement techniques to further refine your social media marketing efforts. With a solid understanding of paid advertising and promotion, you're well-equipped to take your social media marketing to new heights.

Chapter 8:

Analytics and Measurement

- **Tracking Performance Metrics**

In the dynamic world of social media marketing, understanding the impact of your efforts is crucial. Analytics and measurement are the backbone of a successful strategy, enabling you to track performance, identify trends, and make data-driven decisions. This chapter delves into the essential metrics you should track and how to analyze this data to refine your marketing strategy.

- **Key Performance Metrics**

To gauge the effectiveness of your social media campaigns, you need to monitor a range of performance metrics. These metrics fall into several categories, each providing valuable insights into different aspects of your strategy.

- **Engagement Metrics**

Engagement metrics track the interactions between your content and audience. High engagement indicates that your content resonates with your audience, fostering a stronger connection with your brand.

Likes: The number of likes your posts receive. While often considered a vanity metric, likes can indicate initial interest.
Comments: Comments show deeper engagement and provide insights into audience sentiment and feedback.
Shares: Shares amplify your content's reach, indicating that your audience finds it valuable enough to share with their network.
Mentions: Mentions track how often your brand is referenced in posts,

helping you understand brand visibility and sentiment.

- **Reach and Impressions**

Reach and impressions metrics help you understand the visibility and spread of your content.

Reach: The number of unique users that have accessed your content. This metric is crucial for assessing your content's visibility.

Impressions: The overall count of all the times your material is shown, even if no one clicks on it. Impressions provide insights into the potential exposure of your content.

- **Traffic Metrics**

Traffic metrics measure the effectiveness of your social media channels in driving visitors to your website or landing pages.

Clicks: The quantity of times visitors click on links within your articles. Clicks are a direct indicator of interest and the effectiveness of your call-to-action (CTA).

Click-Through Rate (CTR): The percentage representation of the click-to-impression ratio. A greater CTR suggests that the material you have to offer is interesting and pertinent to your readers.

- **Conversion Metrics**

Conversion metrics track the actions users take after engaging with your content, providing insights into the effectiveness of your social media strategy in driving business outcomes.

Conversions: The quantity of desired user actions, like downloads, sign-ups, or sales, that occur. Conversions are the ultimate measure of your campaign's success.

Conversion Rate: The percentage of users who complete a desired action out of the total number of clicks. A higher conversion rate indicates that your landing pages and CTAs are effective.

Cost Per Conversion: The total cost of your campaign divided by the number of conversions. This metric helps you assess the efficiency of your ad spend.

- **Customer Metrics**

Customer metrics provide insights into customer satisfaction, loyalty, and advocacy.

Customer Satisfaction Score (CSAT): A measure of how satisfied customers are with your brand, typically gathered through surveys.

Net Promoter Score (NPS): A measure of customer loyalty and likelihood to recommend your brand to others. To calculate NPS, you ask consumers to rate your brand on a 0–10 scale of likelihood of recommendation.

Customer Lifetime Value (CLV): The total revenue you can expect from a customer over the course of their relationship with your brand. CLV helps you understand the long-term value of your customers.

- **Analyzing Data to Inform Strategy**

Collecting data is just the first step. To truly harness the power of analytics, you need to analyze this data to uncover actionable insights and inform your strategy. Here's how to effectively analyze your social media data:

Setting Benchmarks and Goals

Before diving into data analysis, it's important to establish benchmarks and goals. Benchmarks provide a point of reference for evaluating your performance, while goals help you measure progress and success.

Historical Benchmarks: Analyze your past performance to establish baseline metrics. This helps you understand trends and set realistic goals.
Industry Benchmarks: Compare your metrics to industry standards to gauge your performance relative to competitors.

SMART objectives are defined as Specific, Measurable, Achievable, Relevant, and Time-bound. For example, "Increase website traffic from social media by 20% over the next three months."

- **Identifying Trends and Patterns**

Analyzing trends and patterns in your data helps you understand what's working and what's not. Look for the following:

Content Performance: Identify which types of content (e.g., videos, images, articles) generate the most engagement. Analyze the topics, formats, and posting times that resonate with your audience.

Audience Behavior: Examine how your audience interacts with your content across different platforms. Identify peak engagement times, preferred content types, and common feedback themes.

Campaign Performance: Evaluate the success of individual campaigns by comparing metrics such as reach, engagement, and conversions. Identify high-performing campaigns to replicate successful strategies.

Using Analytics Tools
There are numerous analytics tools available to help you track and analyze

your social media performance. Here are some popular options:

Native Analytics: Most social media platforms offer built-in analytics tools, such as Facebook Insights, Twitter Analytics, Instagram Insights, and LinkedIn Analytics. These tools provide platform-specific metrics and insights.

Google Analytics: Use Google Analytics to track traffic from social media to your website. Set up UTM parameters to track specific campaigns and measure conversions.

Third-Party Tools: Tools like Hootsuite, Sprout Social, and Buffer offer comprehensive social media analytics, allowing you to track performance across multiple platforms in one place.

- **Making Data-Driven Decisions**

Data-driven decisions are critical for optimizing your social media strategy.

Here's how to use your data to make informed decisions:

Optimize Content Strategy: Use engagement metrics to refine your content strategy. Focus on creating more of the content that generates high engagement and less of what doesn't resonate with your audience.

Adjust Posting Schedule: Analyze engagement patterns to determine the best times to post. Plan your content to get the most exposure and engagement.

Refine Targeting: Use audience insights to refine your targeting. Adjust your audience segments based on demographic, interest, and behavior data to ensure your content reaches the right people.

Improve Ad Campaigns: Continuously monitor and optimize your ad campaigns based on performance data. Adjust budgets, targeting, and creatives to improve your ROI.

Enhance Customer Experience: Use customer feedback and sentiment analysis to identify areas for improvement. Address common pain points and enhance the overall customer experience.

- **Reporting and Communicating Insights**

Effectively communicating your insights is crucial for driving action and aligning your team. Here's how to create impactful reports:

Visualize Data: Use charts, graphs, and dashboards to visualize your data. Visual representations make it easier to understand and communicate key insights.

Highlight Key Metrics: Focus on the metrics that matter most to your goals. Highlight key performance indicators and provide context for the data.

Actionable Insights: Go beyond presenting data. Provide actionable recommendations based on your analysis. Clearly articulate the steps needed to improve performance.

Regular Reporting: Establish a regular reporting cadence (e.g., weekly, monthly, quarterly) to keep your team informed and aligned. Regular reports help track progress and identify trends over time.

In conclusion, Measurement and analytics are crucial elements of a successful social media marketing plan. By tracking key performance metrics, analyzing data, and making data-driven decisions, you can continuously optimize your efforts and achieve your marketing goals.

In the next chapter, we'll explore advanced techniques for leveraging influencer partnerships and collaborations to amplify your reach and impact. With a solid understanding of analytics and measurement, you're well-equipped to take your social media marketing to new heights and drive meaningful results for your business.

Chapter 9

Adaptation and Innovation

- **Staying Ahead of Trends**

The only thing that is consistent in the fast-paced world of social media is change. Businesses need to constantly innovate and adapt in order to succeed. Staying ahead of trends is not just about keeping up; it's about anticipating the next big thing and being prepared to pivot when necessary. This chapter will explore the importance of staying current with trends and experimenting with new strategies to maintain a competitive edge.

- **The Importance of Trend Awareness**

Social media trends can significantly impact how businesses engage with their audience. Trends can dictate the types of content that resonate, the platforms that gain popularity, and the methods of interaction that users prefer. Understanding these patterns enables you to:

1. **Engage More Effectively:** By understanding what content and formats are currently popular, you can create more engaging and relevant posts that capture your audience's attention.
2. **Innovate and Differentiate:** Keeping an eye on emerging trends can inspire new ideas and help your brand stand out in a crowded marketplace.
3. **Optimize Performance:** Adapting to trends ensures that your social media strategies remain effective,

helping you achieve better performance metrics and ROI.

- **Tools and Methods for Trend Analysis**

To stay ahead of trends, you need to actively monitor and analyze the social media landscape. Here are a few useful resources and techniques:

1. Social Listening Tools: Platforms like Hootsuite, Sprout Social, and Brandwatch allow you to monitor conversations around specific topics, hashtags, and brands. This helps you identify emerging trends and understand audience sentiment.

2. Trend Reports: Many marketing firms and social media platforms publish regular trend reports. These reports can provide valuable insights into what's currently popular and what's expected to rise.

3. Competitor Analysis: Regularly review the social media activities of your competitors. Analyze their content, engagement rates, and audience feedback to identify successful strategies and trends.

4. Industry News: Follow industry news sources, blogs, and influencers who specialize in social media marketing. They often highlight new trends and provide expert analysis.

5. Data Analytics: Use analytics tools to track the performance of your content and identify patterns. Look for spikes in engagement or shifts in audience behavior that might indicate emerging trends.

- **Adapting to Trends**

Once you've identified a trend, the next step is to adapt your strategy accordingly. Here's how you can effectively incorporate trends into your social media marketing:

1. Content Creation: Adjust your content strategy to reflect current trends. This might involve experimenting with new content formats like live videos, stories, or interactive posts.

2. Platform Focus: If a particular platform is gaining popularity, consider increasing your presence there. For example, if TikTok's user base is growing and aligns with your target audience, it may be worth investing more resources into creating TikTok content.

3. Engagement Tactics: Adapt your engagement tactics to match current trends. For example, if user-generated content is trending, encourage your audience to create and share content related to your brand.

4. Influencer Collaborations: Partner with influencers who are at the forefront of new trends. Their influence can help you reach a broader audience and lend credibility to your brand's participation in the trend.

5. Advertising Strategies: Update your advertising strategies to leverage trending formats and placements. For instance, if vertical videos in stories are performing well, incorporate them into your ad campaigns.

- **Experimenting with New Strategies**

Innovation is key to staying relevant in social media marketing. Experimenting with new strategies allows you to discover what works best for your brand and audience. Here's how to foster a culture of innovation:

- **Encouraging Creativity and Experimentation**

1. Create a Culture of Innovation: Encourage your team to think outside the box and experiment with new ideas. Provide a safe environment where they feel comfortable taking risks and learning from failures.

2. Allocate Resources: Dedicate a portion of your budget and resources to experimentation. This might include testing new platforms, content formats, or engagement tactics.

3. Pilot Programs: Run small-scale pilot programs to test new strategies before rolling them out on a larger scale. This allows you to evaluate their effectiveness and make adjustments as needed.

4. Collaborative Brainstorming: Regularly hold brainstorming sessions with your team to generate new ideas and explore potential strategies. Encourage diverse perspectives to foster creativity.

- **Implementing and Testing New Strategies**

1. Set Clear Objectives: Before implementing a new strategy, define clear objectives and key performance indicators (KPIs). This will help you

measure success and determine whether the strategy is worth pursuing.
2. A/B Testing: Use A/B testing to compare different versions of your content, ads, or engagement tactics. This method allows you to identify which variations perform best and refine your approach.
3. Monitor Performance: Closely monitor the performance of new strategies using analytics tools. Track metrics such as engagement, reach, conversions, and ROI to evaluate their effectiveness.
4. Iterate and Optimize: Based on your analysis, make necessary adjustments to optimize the new strategy. Continuously iterate and refine your approach to improve results.

- **Case Studies of Successful Adaptation and Innovation**

Learning from real-world examples can provide valuable insights and inspiration for your own efforts. Here are a few case studies that demonstrate successful adaptation and innovation in social media marketing:

1. Airbnb's User-Generated Content Campaign: Airbnb capitalized on the trend of user-generated content by encouraging users to share their travel experiences using the hashtag #AirbnbExperiences. This not only increased engagement but also provided authentic content that resonated with their audience.

2. Nike's Use of AR on Snapchat: Nike leveraged augmented reality (AR) on Snapchat to create an interactive experience for users. By allowing users to virtually try on new sneaker models, Nike increased user engagement and drove higher sales.

3. Wendy's Twitter Strategy: Wendy's adopted a bold and humorous tone on Twitter, engaging with users in a way that stood out from typical corporate accounts. This strategy garnered significant attention, increased brand visibility, and improved customer engagement.

In conclusion, Adaptation and innovation are essential for staying relevant and competitive in the ever-evolving landscape of social media marketing. By staying ahead of trends and continuously experimenting with new strategies, you can create a dynamic and effective social media presence that resonates with your audience and drives business results.

In the next chapter, we'll explore how to build and maintain a strong brand identity on social media. With the knowledge and tools to adapt and innovate, you're well-equipped to navigate the challenges and opportunities of the social media world. By embracing change and fostering a culture of creativity, your brand can achieve sustained success and make a lasting impact in the digital realm.

Chapter 10

Case Studies and Success Stories

- **Practical Instances of Successful Social Media Marketing**

To truly understand the potential of social media marketing, it's invaluable to look at real-world examples where businesses have successfully navigated the digital landscape. These case studies highlight innovative strategies, creative campaigns, and the tangible results achieved through effective social media marketing.

- **Nike's "Dream Crazy" Campaign**

Nike has long been a master of compelling storytelling, and their "Dream Crazy" campaign, featuring

Colin Kaepernick, is a prime example. Launched in 2018, the campaign capitalized on the power of controversy and social issues to make a bold statement. Kaepernick, a former NFL quarterback known for kneeling during the national anthem to protest racial injustice, became the face of Nike's message: "Believe in something. Even if it means sacrificing everything."

Results:
- The campaign generated over 2.7 million mentions on social media within the first 24 hours.
- Nike's online sales surged by 31% in the days following the ad's release.
- The campaign won an Emmy for Outstanding Commercial, highlighting its impact and resonance.

Lessons Learned:
- **Boldness Pays Off:** Taking a stand on social issues can polarize

audiences, but it also strengthens brand loyalty among those who share your values.

- **Authenticity Matters:** Authentic messaging that aligns with your brand's identity can create powerful connections with your audience.

- **Airbnb's #WeAccept Campaign**

Airbnb's #WeAccept campaign was launched during the Super Bowl in 2017. The ad, which featured a diverse array of faces and the message "We believe no matter who you are, where you're from, who you love, or who you worship, we all belong," addressed the rising concerns over immigration and inclusivity.

Results:
- The campaign video received over 5 million views on YouTube within the first 48 hours.

- Airbnb experienced a significant increase in bookings and positive brand sentiment.
- The campaign garnered widespread media coverage, enhancing Airbnb's reputation as a socially responsible brand.

Lessons Learned:
- **Timeliness and Relevance:** Addressing current social issues can create a strong emotional connection with audiences.
- **Inclusivity:** Promoting inclusivity and diversity can enhance brand perception and reach a broader audience.

Wendy's Twitter Strategy
Wendy's has become famous for its snarky and humorous Twitter presence. By engaging with followers in a witty and often irreverent tone, Wendy's has successfully differentiated itself from other fast-food chains. Their approach

includes playful roasts of competitors, viral tweets, and real-time interactions with fans.

Results:
- Wendy's has amassed millions of followers on Twitter, with individual tweets often going viral.
- The brand's social media strategy has led to increased brand awareness and engagement.
- Wendy's has maintained a strong and loyal online community, frequently driving sales through social media promotions.

Lessons Learned:
- **Personality Sells:** Developing a unique and consistent brand voice can significantly boost engagement and make your brand memorable.
- **Real-Time Engagement:** Responding in real-time to followers

and trending topics keeps your brand relevant and top-of-mind.

- **Lessons Learned from Notable Campaign.**

Analyzing these and other successful campaigns reveals several key lessons that can be applied to your social media marketing strategy.

- **Embrace Storytelling**

Effective social media campaigns often tell compelling stories that resonate emotionally with audiences. Whether it's a powerful message about social justice, an inspiring personal journey, or a humorous take on everyday life, storytelling can make your content more engaging and memorable.

Tips:

- Identify the core message or theme that aligns with your brand's values and mission.
- Use authentic voices and real-life examples to enhance credibility and relatability.
- Incorporate visual elements like videos, images, and infographics to enrich the storytelling experience.

- **Leverage User-Generated Content**

User-generated content (UGC) can be a powerful tool for building trust and authenticity. Campaigns that encourage users to share their own experiences and content can create a sense of community and amplify your brand's reach.

Examples:
- Starbucks' #WhiteCupContest: Starbucks invited customers to decorate their iconic white cups and share photos on social media. The

contest generated thousands of entries and increased engagement.
- GoPro's UGC Campaign: GoPro frequently showcases videos and photos taken by its customers, demonstrating the product's capabilities and fostering a community of enthusiasts.

Tips:
- Encourage your audience to participate by creating branded hashtags and offering incentives.
- Showcase user-generated content on your social media channels to recognize and celebrate your community.
- Ensure that the UGC aligns with your brand's image and messaging.

- **Utilize Influencer Partnerships**

Collaborating with influencers can help you reach a wider audience and establish your brand's legitimacy. Influencers have established trust with their followers, and their endorsements can drive significant engagement and conversions.

Examples:
- **Daniel Wellington:** The watch brand built its business by partnering with Instagram influencers, who showcased the watches in their posts and offered discount codes.
- **FitTea:** The detox tea brand leveraged influencers across multiple social media platforms to promote their products, resulting in massive brand awareness and sales growth.

Tips:
Select influencers whose followers share the same values as your brand and target market.
- Develop authentic collaborations where influencers can genuinely endorse your products or services.

- Track the performance of influencer campaigns using metrics like engagement, reach, and conversions to evaluate ROI.

- **Measure and Adapt**

Successful campaigns are grounded in data-driven decision-making. Regularly measuring performance and adapting strategies based on insights is crucial for sustained success.

Examples:
- **Oreo's Daily Twist Campaign:** To celebrate its 100th anniversary, Oreo created 100 different ads over 100 days, each reflecting current events. The campaign was continuously adapted based on audience reactions and trends.
- **Netflix's Personalized Marketing:** Netflix uses data analytics to personalize marketing messages and

recommendations, leading to higher engagement and subscriber retention.

Tips:
- Establish clear KPIs and track relevant metrics to evaluate campaign performance.
- Use analytics tools to gather insights and identify areas for improvement.
- Be flexible and willing to pivot your strategy based on data and feedback.

In conclusion, The case studies and success stories explored in this chapter illustrate the transformative power of effective social media marketing. From bold, issue-driven campaigns to humorous and engaging social media strategies, the common thread is a deep understanding of the audience and a commitment to authenticity, creativity, and continuous adaptation.

As you reflect on these examples, consider how you can apply these lessons to your own social media marketing efforts. By embracing storytelling, leveraging user-generated content, utilizing influencer partnerships, and continually measuring and adapting your strategies, you can create impactful campaigns that resonate with your audience and drive meaningful results.

In this ever-evolving digital landscape, staying ahead of trends and fostering a culture of innovation will position your brand for long-term success. With the insights and strategies outlined in this book, you are well-equipped to navigate the challenges and seize the opportunities of social media marketing in 2024 and beyond.

Conclusion

Navigating the Future of Social Media Marketing

As we reach the conclusion of this comprehensive guide, it's essential to reflect on the transformative journey we've undertaken together. From the foundational principles of social media marketing to the intricate strategies of content creation, community engagement, and data-driven decision-making, we've covered the vast landscape of social media marketing with a detailed and insightful approach. This final chapter aims to equip you with a forward-looking perspective, helping you navigate the ever-evolving terrain of social media marketing with confidence and creativity.

- **The Ever-Evolving Landscape**

The world of social media is dynamic and fast-paced. Platforms rise and fall in popularity, new features are constantly introduced, and user behaviors shift. As a marketer, your ability to adapt and innovate is crucial. Staying current with trends and being willing to experiment with new strategies will set you apart from the competition.

- **Embracing Change**

One of the most significant challenges and opportunities in social media marketing is the pace of change. What is effective now might not be tomorrow. This requires a mindset that is open to learning and adaptation. Embrace change not as a hurdle but as a chance to grow and improve.

1. Continuous Learning: Make it a habit to stay updated with the latest trends, tools, and best practices.

Participate in online networks, read industry blogs, and attend webinars.

2. Flexibility: Be prepared to pivot your strategies based on what the data tells you. Flexibility will allow you to respond effectively to shifts in user behavior and platform algorithms.

- **The Power of Authenticity**

In an age where consumers are bombarded with advertising messages, authenticity stands out. Audiences crave genuine connections and transparency from brands. Authentic marketing is not just a buzzword; it's a powerful approach that builds trust and loyalty.

- **Building Trust**

Trust is the cornerstone of any relationship, and this holds true in social media marketing. By being authentic, you show your audience that you value them not just as customers but as individuals.

1. Transparent Communication: Share the story behind your brand, including your values and mission. Be honest about your products or services, and own up to mistakes when they happen.

2. Engagement: Actively engage with your audience. Participate in conversations, answer to remarks, and express gratitude for their support.

- **Harnessing Data and Analytics**

Data is the backbone of effective social media marketing. It provides insights into what's working and what isn't, helping you make informed decisions. Throughout this book, we've emphasized the importance of tracking performance metrics and analyzing data to inform your strategy.

- **Data-Driven Decision Making**

Using data effectively can transform your social media efforts from guesswork to a science.

1. Set Clear Objectives: Define what success looks like for your campaigns. Whether it's increasing brand awareness, driving traffic to your website, or boosting sales, having clear objectives will guide your data analysis.

2. Analyze and Optimize: Regularly review your performance metrics. Look for patterns and insights that can help you refine your strategies. Don't be afraid to test new approaches and learn from the results.

- **Innovation and Creativity**

Innovation is at the heart of successful social media marketing. With so much content competing for attention, creativity is your tool to stand out. Innovative campaigns can capture the imagination of your audience and drive engagement in ways that traditional approaches cannot.

- **Thinking Outside the Box**

Innovation often means stepping outside your comfort zone and trying something new.

1. Creative Content: Experiment with different types of content, from interactive posts and videos to user-generated content and live streams. Creativity can help your brand become memorable.

2. New Platforms: Don't be afraid to explore new social media platforms. While it's essential to have a strong presence on the major platforms, emerging platforms can offer unique opportunities to reach new audiences.

- **Looking Forward**

As we look to the future of social media marketing, several key trends are poised to shape the industry. From the rise of artificial intelligence and machine learning to the increasing importance of personalization and privacy, staying ahead of these trends will be crucial.

- **Future Trends**

1. Artificial Intelligence (AI): AI is transforming social media marketing by enabling more personalized content, improving customer service with chatbots, and providing deeper insights through advanced analytics.

2. Personalization: Consumers expect personalized experiences. Using data to tailor your content and offers to individual preferences will become increasingly important.

3. Privacy and Ethics: With growing concerns about data privacy, marketers must prioritize ethical practices and transparency. Building trust through responsible data use will be essential.

- **Gratitude and Encouragement**

As we conclude this book, we want to extend our heartfelt gratitude to you, our reader. Thank you for embarking on this journey with us, from the basics of social media marketing to the advanced strategies and insights shared in these pages. Your dedication to learning and growing as a marketer is commendable.

Your Feedback Matters

If you've gained something meaningful from this book, we encourage you to share your thoughts and leave a review. Your feedback not only helps us improve but also aids other readers in discovering the value of this resource.

The world of social media marketing is rich with opportunities for those willing to embrace change, harness data, and innovate. With the knowledge and tools provided in this book, you are well-equipped to navigate the complexities of social media marketing and drive meaningful results for your brand.

Remember, the key to success lies in your ability to stay curious, be adaptable, and always prioritize authenticity and creativity in your efforts. As you move forward, may your social media marketing endeavors be fruitful and fulfilling.

Once more, we appreciate your participation in this adventure. We wish you all the best in your social media marketing adventures and look forward to hearing about your successes. Happy marketing!

141